A Way of Loving

RODOLFO DEG. IBAÑEZ, PHD, MD (HC-MMS)

TABLE OF CONTENTS

PROLOGUE

*G*reat things happen when people are in love. Some blush just seeing the person they love. Others simply become breathless. Many wrote about their emotions, their joys and pains of loving, and everything else that makes one want to fall in love.

In my case, I wanted to share not only the emotions of loving, but the larger purpose for which the presence of a greater being is apparent.

I invite you to chance upon the different dimensions of love as I saw it grow in myself, the relationships I nurtured with my family, friends, and workmates, and the community which serves as my own ministry, my Galilee, where the Lord established the beginning of a true Christian community.

It can be true that love stories can be charming. But when the stories are about real people, it can stir something more profound in all of us. Hopefully, the stories you will read will allow something similarly magical to happen to you as well.

It is no surprise that **"A Way of Loving,"** not only transforms but renews the values by which we live by. Truly, a soul-cleansing experience!

The Courage to be Pinoy

CHAPTER 1

Truly Pinoy

⁕ ⁕ ⁕

The Philippines was under colonial rule by the Spaniards for 300 years and by the Americans for another 50 years. Both colonizers left a mark that made us Filipinos feel we are second class citizens in our own country. We were made to believe that anything foreign, whether it be our persons or the goods we produce, are better than local. It took away our pride for ourselves and our country. As a result, Filipinos would rather live in Spain or America or anywhere else, except the Philippines.

The culture of colonial mentality ruled our lives. Even our name Filipino was given a deriding short name. Foreigners who want to belittle us call us Pinoys, a word taken from Fili—**Pino** with letter **Y** added.

But my father is of a different breed. He took pride in being called Pinoy, for his country and for himself, considering it is also his nickname.

My Father was 13 years old when he entered school. He finished the elementary level only in 5 years, even graduating top of his class. His father was a Spanish seaman lost at sea, and was not able to honor his promise to his mother to bring her to the altar.

His mother married a Cebuano, from the Visayan Region in the Philippines. He was an Ybanez, but my Tatay (father) adopted the Spanish surname of Ibanez. I don't know if the change of letter made any difference. I supposed he just wanted to belong to someone equally responsible for his existence even if he never knew him or knew his true surname.

When his stepfather died, who loved him as if he was his own, his dying words were "Pinoy, help your mother, you are now the father of the family. Your brother and sister need you." His eyes blurred with tears, Tatay made a vow and lived up to it.

He was 7 years old when he became head of their family. Every morning, he was in the nearby wet market offering his services. He accepted every pittance they gave him. Afternoons, he tried his luck looking for felled trees in the forest and turned them into charcoal, *"uling"*. His income added food on the table. His mother's earnings as a seamstress was not enough for their needs.

One morning, he noticed his brother and sister preparing for school. He looked out the window and saw children walking at a distance towards the only school in town. It was the first day of classes. He looked at my Lola (grandmother), hesitated, then took courage, *"Inay, ako ba puede rin mag-aral?* (Mom, can I also go to school?)

My Lola did not say anything. She put on her head wrap, took something from a jar and left. When she came back she gave a piece of paper to Tatay. *"Sabi ng Principal puede ka nang pumasok bukas."* (The Principal said you can go to school tomorrow). Then with a naughty smile added, *"saka maligo ka daw, malayo pa na aamoy ka na nya."* (Wash yourself thoroughly, the principal said, he can smell you a mile away), and burst out laughing.

On Tatay's first day of school, he wanted to go home. His age, height, and bulk made a lot of difference to the 6 and 7 year old kids in his class. During breaks they made fun of him, *"Bobo si Pinoy, bobo si Pinoy."* (Pinoy is an idiot, Pinoy is an idiot).

And yet, a few weeks later, everyone noticed, his hand was always raised when a question difficult to answer was asked by the teacher. *"Ano ba mga bata, si Pinoy lang ba ang nagaaral sa inyo?"* (Hey kids is it only Pinoy who studies his lesson?)

On graduation day, this was how the principal introduced him, "To the boy everyone called "idiot," goes the highest honor, our valedictorian, Agripino Atienza Ibanez."

My Lola's heart burst with joy, her son everyone branded *"putok sa buho"* (a bastard) brought her honor.

My father knew there was no way he can go to high school. He needed to help my Lola and high school was in the next town. The offer of scholarship is only for tuition fees and books. Yet, God works in mysterious ways. One day as he was coming out of the forest, all black because of the sack of charcoal on his back, his younger brother running all the way from home, almost out of breath said, *"Kuya,* (endearing word for elder brother) *mayroon higante, hinahanap ka."* (Kuya, a giant is looking for you.)

It turned out the tall American was the superintendent of the only fish canning factory in town. He heard Tatay's valedictory speech and was impressed. "I need someone to oil and clean the machines in the plant. I can only pay one peso and fifty centavos a day. (P1.50 /day). To Tatay that was a fortune. He looked at the tall American, then his brother, and smiled—his dream of becoming an Illustrado, a gentleman, a man of his words, was possible after all!

Mr. Hinckley, the American, became his mentor.

Soon, they were allowing him to handle the simple machines, then, the more complicated ones. The other mechanics saw in him the search for knowledge they found difficult to embrace. When there is a major breakdown, no one can ask him to go home or sleep, much less rest. He just has to solve the problem. His aura was infectious. His actions motivated everyone to put their heads and muscles together to solve the problem.

Before Mr. Hinckley left to be the GM of a gold mine in Paracale, Camarines Norte, my father was already the Chief Mechanic of the Canning factory in town. When WWII broke out, Tatay was superintendent of machineries in the same gold mine where his mentor was.

The war separated them.

In 1945 a few months after Independence Day, Mr. Hinckley found us in Marulas, Polo, Bulacan, and now Valenzuela City. "Pinoy, I am one of those heading a company to help rehabilitate the country. We need engineers. We need you."

"But Mr. Hinckley, I have no degree, you are looking for graduate engineers."

"Don't worry, the war dissipated the line-up of professionals in the country. President Manuel Roxas issued a Commonwealth decree. All experienced technicians will be allowed to take the government examination."

Tatay aced the test. The Philippine Government gave him the license of MECHANICAL PLANT ENGINEER.

At last, his dream to be an ILLUSTRADO has come true. Yet, Tatay's dream is bigger than that! He made sure, all his nine children brought him a college diploma. To him, education is important as hard work to be a success. On his death bed, I promised Tatay I will gift him with a doctorate degree. I fulfilled my promise when I reached 64 years of age and felt I have just begun the fight!

Tatay was a graduate of the "University of Hard Knocked," the best school ever. Can anyone do better!

Truly Pinoy!

Our latest grandchild name Kyle

CHAPTER 2

I Am Lost Without You

❧ ❧ ❧

*T*atay taught me how to love. If there was something he said I should know was keeping his vow of fidelity to Nanay (mother) because there was only one woman in his life. Indeed, he was a one woman man.

I have never seen so much caring and compassion in the way he loved Nanay. It was a love that endured because even when he crossed the great divide, that love continued to stay with Nanay in the way she treated things. How she would fall back to her shell when she heard her children arguing. It was her way of letting us feel that Tatay never raised his voice on her. When she kept to herself, we knew it's a signal to stop. There were better ways to settle our petty differences.

Tatay loved little things. I remember we always had a dog for a pet. There were times when the dog got to eat first before he did. Nanay often chided him because our dog waited under the table for his crumbs; they really were his own share of food so the dog ended up eating more than he did. I recall him never passing-by a lost kitten or a bird that hurt its wings. He was there first, always, to care for them.

If his love for little things was intense, you should see him treat our relatives who were even poorer than we were. He never let them feel they had nothing. They came to our house to get a bite to eat. Because oftentimes they came unannounced, even late in the evening, Nanay usually scrounged for whatever food was left in the kitchen. But our relatives never left without having their fill. Tatay would even give them his last coins for their fare. He was a man intensely in love with life and he made sure we immersed ourselves in the same kind of love in the way we treated whoever cupid brought our way.

There are several women in my life. My Mother, my grandmothers, and my daughters. But most of all there is my wife to whom my devotion is unwavering. To me, Leth, my wife, is not just the mother of my children. She is the keeper of my heart and my very own angel of good fortune. When a friend asked why I love her so much, my answer was simple: in her I found the Mother of our Lord, Mama Mary.

Mary the woman always beside Joseph, never complained. Her love for Joseph and Jesus is one of endless sacrifice. I captured the essence of Mama Mary's love in the first letter of St. Paul to the Corinthians, *"....love is always patient and kind; it is never jealous; love is never boastful or conceited; it is never rude or selfish; it does not take offense, and is not resentful; love takes no pleasure in other people's*

sins but delights in the truth; it is always ready to excuse, to
trust, to hope, and to endure whatever comes...."

It is the same kind of love Leth and I have for each
other. Leth and I had a simple wedding and the reception
even more humble. I had wanted to give her a grander
wedding but both of us agreed to save the money instead.
Our family and friends understood our decision.

The children were the joys of our lives.

We have fond memories of their growing up. We
remember the time when our children began competing
for their mother's attention. With all of them then in
elementary school, they all wanted to be tutored first.
It was usually our eldest daughter, Leah, who laid out
the plans, "*Ma, akong una,* (Me, first Ma) please?" And
our youngest son, Jun would follow, *"Akong* first, Ma, *ako
naman."* (I should be the first this time, Ma)

Carlo, the eldest, just listened knowing that if he got
the last turn, he would have all the time with his mom.
The ride home from school was spent negotiating the
tutoring schedule for the rest of the week. Those were
the times when she felt most needed and fulfilled. Nikki,
our youngest, arrived years after our other children had
grown. She was the luckiest because it wasn't just Leth and
I who spoiled her—her brothers and sister, too.

Leth dropped off the children in school one day when
she happened to glance at the rear view mirror of her car.
That's when she saw our youngest son, running unmindful
of the other cars on the road. He was shouting but she
couldn't make out what he was saying. Thinking the worst,
she put her foot on the brake and rushed out, her heart
pounding, ready to cry.

"Bakit, anak, what's wrong?" (Why son, what's wrong?) she asked. Her boy, in between sobs, replied, *"Ma, nakalimutan mo ang* goodbye kiss *ko"* (You forgot my goodbye kiss).

Leth swears her heart just leaped out of her at that moment. And before she knew it, she was hugging him tightly, crying, and with a gentle tug said, "Sorry akala ko na-kiss na kita" (Sorry, I thought I kissed you already).

I told her it must have been a happy moment. She said happy does not even begin to describe it.

Once Leth starts talking about the children, she couldn't stop. There would be twinkle in her eyes as she tells about a time when the entire family ate out for dinner. While waiting, they started playing a game, making sounds of different animals. It was her turn. In excitement, she blurted out, "The pig says bow wow, wow!" like a dog barking. Everyone roared in laughter. She immediately caught the folly of her remark. Joining in her children's laughter was the entire restaurant.

We have more stories of our children. A personal favorite is our biking adventures—an activity we all loved to do together as a family. When we moved to our first house in the South, we decided to spend our weekends biking to explore different places. Carlo, as always, is ahead of us as we try to maneuver between the potholes and rocks that has become the familiar challenge on the winding path of Moonwalk Subdivision in Paranaque. Carlo would never be in any other spot other than in the lead. At an early age, I already saw the burning desire in him to always want to be the first, and to come on top, no matter what.

Jun, our youngest son, was assigned to keep the pace. He does not push too hard but instead, puts himself in rhythm with Carlo so we all could keep a steady speed. Leth and Leah are at the tail-end as I stay on the side making sure everyone is safe. Our first stop is always the bakery. The taste of Pepsi washed away our burning throats as we gulped the ice cold drink. We chat a while to plan the rest of the trip. The children would plot our next best route.

And then our ride back home would always end up in a race. There is no formal challenge but the competitive spirit has always been a part of our family. It has shaped our children and has been the key in their growing up years. Between Carlo, Leah and Jun, the race takes place very naturally. I would stay back. Sometimes, I bike ahead when the roads become a little bit tricky. And then I'll pull back again when it's safe. Moonwalk at that time was still surrounded by rice fields. From a far distance, the roof of our house would loom. The children's speed heightens as we near home. And often, Carlo would nose them. Other times, Jun would. Leah would finish first only when her brothers are feeling kind and generous.

I look back on these biking memories with my children often. Especially when we spend vacation days together, time that always seem short. When it is time for everyone to go back to work I would feel loneliness in my heart.

The children were entering college when the country's political situation worsened. It was time to make a difficult decision. With heavy hearts, we decided to send our children abroad to finish college. Having to say goodbye was painful but it had to be done for the children's sake.

Leth missed the children terribly. And while we spent most of our time doting on Nikki, our youngest child, still, the elder children's absence was hard for us.

It was God who opened a window for us. Amidst the political upheaval rocking the government, we were fortunate to find a quiet place to spend our weekends, far away from the threat of a shooting war. As our farmhouse was being built, we were slowly welcomed to the community. The people were warm and friendly, especially the children. They would gather the wood chippings and wood dust to help clean up. They also brought water for the carpenters. Leth cooked and they would eat under the big acacia tree.

One time, I came home after a round of golf in the nearby country club. I heard familiar laughter in the dining room. Thinking that our children came home to surprise us, I was heartened to see that it was the children in the farm. They were finally eating with her inside the house.

That evening, while we were in bed, she gently nudged me, "Dad, I'd like to send those kids to school, *pwede ba?*" (can I?)

Saying yes was the best decision we ever made.

The reaching out to our new community created a new beginning in the farm. Let me tell you of how our chapel came about. She had no professional help. She worked only with her dream, her heart, and those she trusted in our farm. She took time to review several pictures of churches around the country. Armed with determination, she sketched the chapel from them.

From a distance, it looks like a regular church. Its adobe stone finish gives a massive appearance yet picturesque in its nature. The facade is faithful to the Paoay Church in

Ilocos whose history goes back to the Spanish times. Yet when you go inside, it feels like the different missions in California. Bahay Maria is what we named our chapel. She gave this name which was also in my mind. That's how it is with us; we think and say the same things most of the time.

A dated Holy family carving hangs on one side across the image of Our Lady of Guadalupe. A Santo Nino stands beside her with a rough wooden crucifix. Natural light gives radiance and brilliance when you are inside.

What drove Leth to build this chapel? She simply wanted more people in our farm to connect with Jesus through the Holy Family. For Leth, the Holy Family is built and founded on true love. Remember, Mother Mary says yes to God in obedience and love. Joseph stands by Mary out of love and obedience to God's will. Jesus is obedient to Joseph and Mary out of love for them and for his father in heaven. Mary is patient and conscientious in raising Jesus whom she loves with all her heart. In Calvary, Mary suffers terribly upon seeing her son on the cross but remains obedient to God's plan...all for love. (365 Days with the Lord)

Saint Jose Maria Escriva, in his book "Furrow" says, "Some people know nothing about God because no one has talked about Him in terms they can understand."

Leth's touch is for people to know God better. Everywhere she goes Leth exhibits a kind of love that is caring, a love that nurtures relationship. The love I have for her comes from another dimension. My love is as strong and reliable as a mother's love, but delicate and trusting as well. Our love story has spanned more than fifty years with four loving children and nine adoring grandchildren. Our love is a romance told in many beautiful and incomplete fairy tales. But I already know that it will finish with a happy ending.

And now, Leth and I are faced with the greatest challenge of our lives. This condition I am facing where life seems to stand still, sapping my energy and spirit. ... I KNOW GOD IS CALLING. ... IT IS TIME!

Yet, we hope. ... Fr Joe, my spiritual director, shared this beautiful message about Faith, Hope, and Love, "You asked for strength and God gave you difficulties to make you strong. You asked for wisdom and God gave you problems to solve. You asked for prosperity and God gave you brains and skills to work. You asked for courage and God gave you danger to overcome. You asked for love and God gave you troubled people to help. You asked God for favors and God gave you opportunities. You received nothing you wanted...but received everything you needed."

Because God is a God of Faith, a God of Hope, and the greatest of all, He is a God of Love.

CHAPTER 3

"A Defensive Church Will Not Inspire and Ignite Souls"

❧ ❧ ❧

I am now in the twilight of my years. But my love affair with the Lord is never ending.... Actually, it didn't start that way. This love affair begun as a puppy love seeking understanding of the strange feeling I have whenever I glanced at the image of Jesus Christ. No one told me of a God that loves me since I was in the womb of my mother.

I always knew my father was a pillar of strength. Like most children who idolize their father, he was like Superman to me. Invincible, indestructible, could do anything he set his mind on.

Yet, his armor had one kink in it. My father was not my first teacher in my studies of the ways of the Lord. I am not saying he was a non-believer, far from it. For everything

I saw in him was only what is good. He had only comforting words for everyone even if there were times people would say not so nice things about him. "Don't mind them," he would tell me, "what is important is what you do. When you put your hand above your chest and you can truly say that you have not done anyone wrong, then be at peace with yourself. Soon enough people will know the truth.

My search for a better understanding of my faith had brought me many doubts. I feared losing my belief in God entirely because of this. I was too young to understand the concept of God. It was strange and overwhelming for a child like me, especially since no one in my family talked about it. Dad and Mom never brought us to Mass on Sundays. I was already in the second grade but neither the school nor the parish priest ever urged us to join catechism lessons. It could be because of the neighborhood tattlers who referred to religion as only for the old or womenfolk. The men who frequented the church were considered sissies.

The 300 years of Spanish colonization brought Christianity to the country but at the same time, it didn't. Religion was conveyed to the natives not to uplift them, but rather, to keep them in bondage. The Spanish conquistador, together with the friars, saw fit to spread religion only to their advantage. So there were more superstitions than truths that the people practiced.

On Good Friday, for example, they were told that one shouldn't take a bath for Jesus was dead. But if you insisted, you had to buy some sort of dispensation from the parish priest to enjoy a bath without committing sin. Eating meat was allowed during Holy Week when one paid the required dispensation. This was what the Spanish taught us. Men could keep their macho reputation by not being seen in church or praying too much. And if they must attend Mass, they should be out smoking during homily which was considered useless anyway since the priest would just ask for donations for the Church. And don't forget, prayers were reserved only for those who wore skirts.

I have a grandmother from my mother's side who made sure that I understood who God is and why I was created. Because of her, I developed my own concept of God and religion. The greatest way by which God showed us his goodness was creating us with spiritual and immortal souls capable of sharing in his love and happiness. God has given young children pure hearts. But as they begin to do wrong by cheating and lying, their hearts begin to grow black dots. And unless these sins are confessed, the devil will one day take over the souls of those whose hearts have turned completely black.

It was a concept easy enough for me to understand and remember. I understood the meaning of my relationship with God as she explained; she was a zealous and self-effacing catechist. She also made sure we knew how to pray the holy rosary. She told us that the rosary is one of the most beautiful prayers of the Church. It wasn't supposed to be boring or repetitious as some claim it to be since the holy rosary conveyed God's message of love and forgiveness because the rosary is a meditation on the life of Jesus—from his birth to his growing-up years, to his proclamation of God's kingdom, and finally his passion, death, and resurrection.

And then the Americans came and brought with them a different kind of religion. They reeducated us about the sanctity of the confessional box. They explained how it wasn't too long ago when the confessional box was said to be the reason why the revolution for independence was exposed. Rumor has it that one of the Katipunan women confessed to a priest about the impending revolt. The priest, fearing for their lives, allegedly violated the sacredness of the confession and reported what he heard in the confessional box to the authorities. In no time, the leaders of the insurrection faced the firing squad of the Guardia Civil. Hundreds of lives were lost. That indiscretion delayed the declaration of Philippine independence.

The Americans were saying theirs was the better religion. Not only did it preach the Ten Commandments in practical ways, it also made it easy for everyone to obey. According to them, their religion did not excommunicate or ban people from church services just because they had practices that the Catholic Church did not promote. Neither did they want you confessing to a minister when in fact, you could just speak directly to God. In any case, your beliefs are just between you and him. And while they recognized the Blessed Virgin to have given birth to Jesus, she was just that and nothing more. To pray for her intercession was unnecessary for only Jesus can save and that he is the only way to God. Saints are just like you and me, they are only humans so they do not possess any special privileges. That was what religion should be all about, according to the Americans.

Now I was really confused. I didn't know who was right. Yet, my innocent heart was yearning to believe in something even if the thought of it was still unfathomable.

For years no one questioned the teachings of the Catholic Church. The Philippines is the only Christian country in Asia. 80% of the 100 million Filipinos are Catholic, but the church is under attack.

I did not vote for President Rodrigo Duterte. Though, I support his war against drug and criminality. His tirade against the perceived "faults" of the leadership of the Catholic Church give me discomfort. The Church is not perfect, almost on a day to day basis we are confronted with discouraging posture of some of the bearer of the Word of God. After more than 2000 years the Church is still evolving, finding the best way to attune itself to the changing times, without sacrificing the doctrines that makes it the true Church founded by Jesus Christ.

We are fortunate that in our path towards "the road less travelled" we can be guided with understanding of where the church stand on certain teachings and hopefully provide us with a well-formed conscience by what the church stands for and not by mistakes committed by its leaders.

The challenge is how to keep our balance when the very person guiding us toward the right path seem to go astray himself. Often, we look at our priest as personification of God because in our mind they are the perfect symbol of the conveyor of God's message. And so the picture of the perfect image of "God" is blurred by our perception that the bearer of God's image is not perfect after all.

Many times confusion arises when in our desire to seek answers to what is ailing us, another man of the clothe encourages us to take a step back and remove ourselves from the source of our pain, exactly what my friend John did, just like President Duterte, by denying the existence of all forms of organized religion.

John related to me his meeting with an elderly Jesuit priest. At the start of their meeting, the kindly Jesuit corrected John when he apologized to the priest for disturbing his retirement. "John, you must know that we priests do not really retire, in fact I am tempted to say – we cannot retire. When we took our vow in the Holy Orders, we committed ourselves in the service of our Lord for a lifetime. As you know Jesus Christ called himself as the Bridegroom. On earth the relationship between the bridegroom and the bride is on a "till death do us part basis". I am afraid that does not apply to us priests. We are on call even in our next life in heaven."

During the course of their conversation, John asked the Jesuit whether not subscribing to organize religion is a sin. To which the priest replied: "Sin can be described as a conscious, responsible and deliberate act of the will, by which, recognizing the existence of a moral choice, one chooses wrong, knowing it to be wrong, because, for the moment, at any rate, it is desired more than its alternative. You were traumatized by your previous encounters with certain religious groups and individuals. I do not fault you for your present attitude towards what you call organized religion."

The priest continued: "I believe that at present you have this very strong stirring in your soul, and because of what you have experienced, you are very much confused where this is pulling you. Allow me to share with you what Her Majesty Queen Elizabeth II said in a special assembly of her group the Anglican Church which she heads: "If we have faith and courage to seek it, we shall be shown new truths in the Gospel of real and immediate relevance to our own time, and we shall be given new insight to understand the problems which arise, almost every day at home and abroad."

Pope Francis without touching the doctrines of the Church is creating a lot of waves. His position on same sex marriages is glaring yet the humanity of his approach silences the sound of those that critics' his position. Our own Bishop Socrates Villegas President of CBCP said, "We are seeing a world in transition and the Church in transition with society.... There are accidentals; spiritual wisdom is knowing what we can and cannot change. ... Families and religion have become shell institutions, but inside has radically change. We still carry the shell but the shell can be deceptive, and fictitious. ... a DEFENSIVE CHURCH WILL NOT INSPIRE AND IGNITE SOULS. ... Our generation of young Catholics seeks Pokemon in our parish churches and accidentally finds God while window shopping. The unconventional mass schedules at noon or late at night are attracting many young Catholics."

Pope Francis, teaches that "Faith is always a cross.... this powerfully echoes Galatians 2:19, where St Paul tells us that he has been crucified with Christ so that now it is Christ Who lives with him, and Colossians 3:3 where he applies this to us: "For you have died, and your life is hidden with Christ in God."

When it comes to faith, I encourage everyone to willingly entertain doubts and uncertainties about it, especially if it is going to bring about a deeper understanding of your relationship with God. You may think that such transgressions may offend God, but these are still far better than the injustices people commit towards one another. Besides, faith is a gift deeply rooted in reason.

I was meditating on this teaching of Pope Francis last Christmas when my friend John once more loomed large in my mind. Despite my hesitancy to greet him that Christmas day, considering he no longer believe in any form of organized religion, I decided to text him anyway:

Hi John,

I don't know if it's still appropriate to greet you Merry Christmas because the word connotes belief in God who freed us from the sin of Adam and Eve. I wrestled with this thought all day. Finally I decided it will do no harm to greet the one person who helped me so much in writing the stories that reflect on the word of God. Merry Christmas my friend for whatever good it brings you and let me apologize if somehow the greeting offends your sensibilities. Thanks.

He texted back immediately:

Hi Rudy,

I'd be very much hurt if the one person who is leading me to the fold, (not that I left it. Not in a million light years!), did not greet me on Christmas Day. I know I commented that even the Evangelists did not agree on Jesus' true birth date. I hasten to say that that is not crucial to me. What is; is that He came in human form, with all His frailties, warts and boils. He can then empathize with mortals like me, and forgive me for my human failings. I quarrel with organized religion and its purported system. Of course system is a must in our affairs lest anarchy takes over. But a system is there to serve and not be the master. It must create doorways and entrances to Jesus' advocacies. This system must not be held back, and be overcome by traditional expectations. The author, A. C. Lewis wrote: "We may ignore, but we can nowhere evade the presence of God."

"We will not 'spend' Christmas.....nor 'observe' Christmas. We will 'keep' Christmas -- keep it as it is.... in all the loveliness of its ancient traditions, may we keep it in our hearts that we may be kept in its hope. I wish you a Blessed Christmas....

For years now I have been guided by my spiritual director and mentioned him time and again to John. So, I called him, "Hi John, Fr. Joe asked about you. May I tell him you are ready to meet?

"Yes."

His reply was music to my ears.

My love affair with the Holy Trinity and Mama Mary is forever. My wife, my family and I are faced with the greatest challenge ever. I have accepted that my condition can only be cured by the Lord!

CHAPTER 4

Friends Forever!

✐ ✐ ✐

*F*unny thing about love God made it so that it is all around. Just look at the people on the street, your neighbors when you find time to say hello, or even stranger in the unlikeliest off places.

St Josemaria, the saint of ordinary life said it well, "To sow, the sower went out—scatter the seeds, apostolic souls. The wind of grace will bear it away if the furrow where it falls is not worthy—sow and be certain that the seed will take root and bear fruit.

The words of Khalil Gibran, the Libyan poet is worth contemplating:

> "And let your best be for your friend. If you must
>   know the ebb of your tide,
> Let him know its flood also.
> For what is your friend that you should seek him
>   with hours to kill?
> Seek him always with hours to live. For it is his to
>   fill your need, but not your emptiness.

And in the sweetness of friendship let there be
laughter, and sharing of pleasures.
For in the dew of little things the heart finds its
morning and is refreshed."

*Phoebe is on my left, Boy, her husband, is on the right
of Leth. This was one of the dinners we had during
Valentine's Day.*

I closed my eyes and memories begin to flood my mind. Forty years is a long time. I notice the raindrops tapping on the window. How soothing it is to hear the drip of rain like the sound of flute. I mumbled prayers for Phoebe and Boy, who took their trip to heaven, and with a parting wish asked them to say hello to Mom and Dad.

We were neighbors. We moved to a modest bungalow in Moonwalk Village during the martial law years. The village were occupied by employees and young professionals beginning to build a career. Boy and Phoebe lived across the street. Boy was managing a car dealership and Phoebe was an ophthalmologist in her Makati clinic, doubling as a pediatrician in our subdivision. They have four girls and a boy. We have two boys and two girls.

Like most friendships, ours started slow. We wanted to make sure positive vibes will surround us. We wanted to see if we will click as friends and if we don't we will at least be nodding friends. But our children just jumped into it without pretensions. On that summer, the Caption's and the Ibañez' children spent time together and studied with the same piano teacher.

Our boys are athletic. A basketball half-court at the back of our house gave them the chance to develop their playing skills. One late Sunday afternoon, the kids challenged me to a game. I was big and tall for them so, two-on-one evened up the game. Carlo, our eldest stuck to me like an NBA guard, freeing his brother, Jun, to take jump shots at will or drive to the hoop. I had the advantage on the rebound because of my bulk. The game was pretty even. I was dribbling to the goal with Carlo, sticking to me like glue, when I felt a sting on my left eye.

Jun exclaimed, *"Dad nagdudugo and mata mo* (Dad, your eye is bleeding)." We walked over to Phoebe with blood and perspiration all over me. She placed gauze over my eye. Leth, heard of the accident, followed with a towel.

Phoebe said, "We have to go to the hospital." She couldn't stop the bleeding unless she operated. She has the most delicate hands I've ever known. Even with the anesthesia, I still felt her assuring soothing voice. She kept a running conversation, *"Rudy, maswerte ka sa puti lang ng mata ang sugat. Mas madali sana tayong natapos kundi dahil sa dumi. Kuko yata ni Carlo ang nakatama* (Rudy, you're lucky, the wound is only in the white portion of your eye. If not for the dirt, we would have finished faster. I think it was Carlo's nail that caused the wound.)"

After a few days, she had to clean the wound. I walked to her clinic. She applied a tetracycline ointment on my eye. I mumbled, "Phoebe, *hindi ako makahinga* (Phoebe, I can't breathe)," and lost consciousness. I do not know how long I was out. As I was falling down, Boy walked into the clinic and caught me. Phoebe grabbed an adrenaline ampule, and gave me the shot. The sting of the needle woke me up. All these happened in seconds. Her presence of mind saved me.

The incident was a blessing in disguise. That was the beginning of our beautiful and enduring friendship. Occasionally, Leth would send them delicacies. They sent us sweet lanzones from their farm. Our friendship grew. Leth is Godmother to Joy, their second girl, and Phoebe is Godmother to our youngest, Nikki.

Phoebe gave me a bit more attention with products she prescribes. I was with Unilab then and while she never sacrificed her patients, when needed she never hesitated writing them. *"Alam mo Rudy, ngayon bago ako sumulat ng reseta, iniisip ko muna ang producto ng* Unilab (You know, Rudy, before I write my prescriptions, I think of Unilab's products first)."

That is how close we became, our Filipino values of *hiya* (shame), *pakikisama* (camaraderie), and *utang ng loob* (being beholden) cemented our friendship. In many instances I went out of my way to make her feel our spirit of Bayanihan (working together). Small things like a ticket to a concert or accommodation when attending medical conventions or just making sure she is on my Christmas list are things Phoebe treasures.

On weekends when I was not on a trip, we biked with the children exploring the different areas near our place which was connected by shallow creeks and narrow pathways. We would stop by a small bakery or sari-sari store to take a drink. Our children enjoyed these adventures the most.

In one of our sorties, we decided to leave the children as we wanted to try to find a safe way to reach Luneta, a beautiful park along Manila Bay. During those times, traffic was already bad and we did not want to endanger the children. At Luneta, disaster struck. We were arrested because our bikes did not have any plate numbers!

At the precinct, my wife and Phoebe confronted the arresting officer, *"Bakit ba kami ang hinuhuli nyo ay samantalang napakarami ng magnanakaw at mamamatay tao na dapat ninyong unahin* (Why arrest us when there are so many thieves and criminals you should attend to first)?"

The officer got peeved, asked us to follow him to the nearest cell, "Ayan po ang mga magnanakaw at mamamatay tao na sinasabi nyo, gusto po ba ninyo isama namin kayo sa kanila" (Here are the thieves and criminals you are talking about, do you want us to put you there?)

Boy is a good judge of character, he knows how turn a losing proposition, into a good hand. He apologized and requested to give us a break. The officer smiled and said, "Medyo kausapin nyo ang asawa nyo at sabihin nyo sa kanila na bawasan ang taray (talk to your wives and tell them to hold their tongues.)"

The experience was one of the milestones in our friendship. For forty years, without fail, we re-energized our relationship on Valentine's Day. The first time we went out was on us. The next year was their turn. We have been alternating every year since then.

A few years back Boy remarked, "Rudy, nakita na natin lahat ng show mula kay Katy dela Cruz, sa lahat ng foreign talents na nagpunta dito, to the present crop of entertainers. Medyo sawa na ako, puede ba mag-isip ka naman ng iba (Rudy, we've seen all the shows from Katy dela Cruz, and all the foreign talents that came here. I'm a bit on my neck with them, can you think of other things)?"

"Alam mo Boy ang gusto lang natin ay magkwentuhan, bakit hindi na lang tayo pumunta sa isang fine restaurant." (You know, Boy, we just want to spend time with each other, why don't we just go to a fine restaurant.). We did.

Our friendship followed God's teaching, "What you sow is what you reap." We planted sincere relationships and harvested sincere friends, friends forever.

"And let your best be for your friend.

If you must know the ebb of your tide, let him know its flood also.

For what is your friend that should seek him with hours to kill?

Seek him always with hours to live.

For it is his to fill your need, but not your emptiness.

And in the sweetness of friendship let there be laughter, and sharing of pleasures.

For in the dew of little things the heart finds its morning and is refreshed."

Ah! Friendship you are truly God's gift!

Lino is at the 2nd row from the right.

CHAPTER 5

The Man Called Lino

❧ ❧ ❧

And then there is Lino, a man most loved in Unilab, a Philippine pharmaceutical company that is the envy of multi-national companies. Lino began his career as general manager of one of the largest companies in Unilab, called Westmont, Inc. Later, he took the responsibility as head of all the marketing companies.

According to Sigmund Freud, psychological forces influencing people's behavior are largely unconscious and that a person cannot fully understand his or her own motivation. When you analyze Freud's theory more carefully you will find that those who have a knack for understanding human behavior can motivate people beyond their capacity to perform. History has shown how some people with the right story to tell could move crowds to get them to act almost with boundless energy especially when they reach the point where achievement is just an eye-wink away.

This brings me to the story of "WE ARE OR WE ARE NOT."

It was the period of Westmont's history when because of the strong emotional bond that held the sales and office people together; they found themselves pulled like magnets to meet in the office at the end of the day and just chat. Sometimes, some people would bring pancit (noodles), others pandesal (bread), and others just peanuts to munch. When Lino would notice them gathering in the conference room, he would order soft drinks and exchange pleasantries with them.

In one of these casual get-togethers, a PSR (professional service representative) started strumming his guitar with the chords of "Battle Hymn of the Republic." Another one with a good voice followed the tune and added lyrics to it. It went like this:

"Lino Imperial is the maker of great men."

He just kept on singing the lyrics over and over again, and then the group caught on and began to sing together following the lead voice. Their sounds were accompanied by clapping of hands. Lino signaled them to stop. Then he requested the guitarist to play the tune again. Slowly he sung:

"Westmont Division we are always on the go, Westmont Division we are always on the go, Westmont Division we are always on the go, we are or we are not."

Slowly they repeated the words trying to fit them to the tune and, as they got used to the lyrics and the tempo, began singing with gusto. You can imagine how energized everyone was, so much that it was almost ten in the evening when they separated. All that time, they sang the song composed on the spot by Lino until their voices were hoarse. Hence, the legendary message, "We are or we are not," meaning we are either great performers or we are not, no ifs and buts!

And the legend continues... Tom Morris, in his book "If Aristotle Ran General Motors," says that in leadership the one and only virtue is nobility: "People are inspired over the long run only by their sense of nobility in who they are and what they are doing. If you can convey a sense of nobility to the people around you, you can unlock their deepest potential. If you can tap into your own sense of nobility, you gain from that the determination and persistence to initiate any important changes that need to be made, and you can stick with the process in good spirit through all the difficulties you may encounter along the way. A sense of nobility in what they are doing will go far toward encouraging people to do the right thing for positive corporate spirit."

In the early years, Unilab's marketing divisions, both ethical and proprietary, reported only to one head, Lino. Once a week, he would call us together to chat. This regular get-together became the forerunner of the PROMOTIONS COMMITTEE or PROCOM for short. During his time, it was one of the more effective ways of creating togetherness among us and developing a sense of belonging. I was barely four months as head of Medichem, one of the newer companies of Unilab, and was the youngest division head at the time.

Looking back, I'd like to believe that the weekly powwows Lino organized was meant for the group to hasten my inclusion into the team of GMs. Our group are battled tested in people management. The group's style was a cross between the Chairman of the Board's easy-to-get-along style and Lino's strict but-full-of-humor-type of leadership. It wasn't too long before I felt I was already one of them.

In one of these weekly chats, the topic of our conversation happened to be about the occurrence of the first total eclipse in Manila two decades back. Everyone were sharing their whereabouts and I could tell that all of them were already working with the company. As I was listening, trying to recall everyone's specific story, someone, Buddy Dolatre, GM of UAP, our considered Dean, asked me point blank: *"Ikaw Rudy, saan ka inabutan ng eclipse* (You Rudy, where were you when the eclipse happened)?"

Thinking my background was so little compared to theirs, I timidly replied, "Third year high school *ako*, chief (I was in third year high school then, chief)." I couldn't understand why, but everyone around the table burst into loud guffaws banging their tables as if to say, "Touché."

After the laughter subsided, one of them came over to my chair (Jun Sanchez, former GM of Westmont) and tapped me on the shoulder, "Okay *ka Rudy, naisahan mo si* Dean (You're okay, Rudy, you put one over the Dean)."

Apparently, the pet peeve of the Dean was talking about age and everyone thought that because of my naiveté I had put one over the Dean without making him feel bad. I remember that incident distinctly because since then I felt everyone treated me with more acceptance. Of course, thanks to Lino and his weekly chats.

In managing us, Lino had a style all his own. You could expect that any program or projects you presented to him would initially meet with a NO! It is not an uncommon experience that when you step out of his room after making an attempt to seek approval of your program, you get the usual comment of people waiting outside with a greeting of *"Nakailang no ka,?"* (How many NOs did you get)?"

It must have been because of Lino's incisive mind that halfway through your presentation, he already knew where you're headed, and if it were nowhere, he would abruptly stop the discussion and give you zero rating. And he would not even say anything, much less explain. He would just ask you to rework your program.

Being new in the marketing's inner chamber, I decided to completely ignore everything I heard and sent him a copy of Medichem's marketing campaign with the note attached; "Sir, Please review at your convenience and I hope I can get some of your time after a week."

The week had gone and no message from him. I called up his secretary and he too said nothing. I requested him to connect me to Lino. Lino just said to pick up the folder from Dan, his secretary. Nothing more.

I reworked the presentation and sent it back. After a week, again nothing. I decided to go to his secretary and pick up my work. It took me almost another three weeks reviewing and analyzing the project before I had the courage to send it back. I was in the middle of a meeting when I received a call from his office. He said to come over and pick up my program so I could put it into effect.

Before I left his office, I learned a lesson I will never forget. "Rudy," he said to me, "the first presentation you gave me, I knew right away you were thinking like a marketing director, the second, you were almost there. Ah! But the third, the program is like a work of art, you were thinking like a real general manager."

Throughout our organization, both domestic and international, you will find men carved in the image of Lino, charismatic leaders with fire burning in their bellies. They are leaders who fight in the front-line with their men. Because they lead their men in battle, it is not unusual that the first bullet fired by the enemy hits them. These men know that their leader is willing to die for them. And they too are willing to die for their leaders. This bond that they have is sealed by their passion and commitment. Lino has a way of sealing this bond.

Tom Morris, talks about religion and public policy, policies that affect the private sector. He had struggled to articulate his feelings and the more he did, the more he saw the individual's insignificance in God's great scheme of things and yet it was this particular insight that made him feel bigger and more important all the time. Morris talks about his encounter with a Rabbi who understood clearly what he was feeling and gave him an ancient piece of Hasidic wisdom that captures well what he was trying to say: "A man should always wear a garment with two pockets. In one pocket, there should be a note, which reads, "I am but dust and ashes." In the other pocket, there should be a paper, which says, "For me, the world was created."

We were preparing for a long weekend breather. That Saturday morning, the whole PROCOM met with our key marketing people to discuss Unilab's marketing plans, get their comments, modify them if necessary, and call for a big rally of our people to launch the program. As usual, Lino was at his best. He deviated from his usual humor and green jokes to establish rapport with us. While there was fire in his voice, we sensed a deep serenity in his talk. He actually talked about life, how in our desire to win material things, we do this at the sacrifice of our soul.

All of us felt the sincerity of his voice, some even began to have moist eyes and everyone was looking at each other with questioning gazes as if asking, "Is this the Lino we know?" He went on to exalt the Lord and asked us to offer this coming campaign to God, then enjoined everybody to give our best so that our offerings will bring greater glory to the Lord.

At the end of his message he spoke of the Rosary and the meaning of the Mysteries. He said the Rosary is like our life. The Joyful Mystery represents the growing years when we try to learn and absorb as much as we can hoping that these years will prepare us to understand and appreciate the true meaning of the Luminous mysteries which is the time of our life when we are able to conquer everything we dare do, such as having a successful marriage, raising our children well, accomplishing a meaningful career that allows us to provide financial security to our family, growing in our professional endeavors and above all sharing our gains, wherever they are with our community. When we do this, he continued, the Sorrowful Mysterious became an anticipation of new beginnings because the Passion and Death of Jesus Christ leads us to the Resurrection which is the time of the Glorious Mysteries the stage of our life, where the Lord is closest to us.

Our reaction to his talk was instantaneous. The room exploded with our hands clapping without end. Many of us were crying. The macho ones who ordinarily would not be affected by such emotions cried the most. Everyone left the room red in the eyes.

That weekend at the height of his career, Lino died. No one was prepared for his dying. At the emergency room all the doctors did their best to revive him. His wife and eldest daughter were by his side talking to him trying to bring him back to life. "Dad," Jojo cried, "Wake up, Mom is here. Your friends from Unilab are here. We are all here, wake up, Dad, wake up."

But Lino's time has come. Dr. Conrado Dayrit, Unilab's head of medical research, gave the news to his wife. "Everyone did their best. It is now more than two hours that the doctors have been pumping his heart with no response. The doctors will continue for as long as you wish it."

Ma'am Betty looked at Ading asked, "Is there still a chance?" Dr. Dayrit shook his head.

Mrs. Imperial finally said, "Let him go. God needs him."

In the funeral, everyone, led by his Westmont boys, were singing:

> Lino Imperial is a maker of great men,
> Lino Imperial is a maker of great men,
> Lino Imperial is a maker of great men,
> We are or we are not!

Lino was the kind of teacher everyone should have. More than a superior, he was a good coach. His beliefs, philosophy, teaching, and wisdom went beyond managing markets and products. His ultimate goal was to bring out the best in you, in all areas of your life.

He was a master of motivation and psychology. He shared his wisdom unselfishly. While he took pride in the accomplishments that you gained as a result of his guidance, he would never claim credit for what you had achieved. Instead he would even go out of his way to talk about your victories.

In 1971, Lino gave me the chance to head Medichem Inc. In 1976, he took me as his direct assistant in marketing, helping him manage all the divisions. Not satisfied with that, he recommended me to hold a position higher than where he was, that of executive vice president and general manager of Unilab, aware that our roles would reverse.

On the day I took over my new responsibility, sometime in 1979, he was the proudest of them all. For Lino was like that, a humble teacher, a loving husband, a caring father, and above all, a faithful brother to Jesus our Lord. Lino, we all miss you.

And we love you!

This is our family that joined the Marian pilgrimage.
Jun is at the left last row

CHAPTER 6

Meeting Pope Francis in a Wheelchair

❧ ❧ ❧

At the end of Lino's message he spoke of the Rosary and the meaning of the Mysteries. He said the Rosary is the guide to a life that please the Lord and complete itself when we finally feel the Lord's embrace as we are welcome in heaven.

On earth we mirror his teachings in our day to day living. I remember the time when my wife and I celebrated our 50th wedding anniversary. Leth, my wife invited all our children together with their love mates to join us in a Marian pilgrimage. I hesitated to come. Even then my asthma is a bother and I lose air taking long walks. To reassure me, my son Jun, promised to bring along a wheel chair.

So, I went to Rome, the first leg of our trip, not really wheezing along but seated on a wheelchair slowly moving. To my joy, the wheelchair turned out to be a magic wand. At the airport the wheels got me preferred check-in status

as well as at the long lines of immigration and boarding....
with my entire family in tow. What better way to start this
trip than being first?

As registered pilgrims, we had tickets for an audience
with the Pope. If we want to be seated near him we have
to line up as early as 4:00 AM. No one seems to want to
wake up that early what with the jet lag and all. We left the
hotel much later since Pope Francis scheduled appearance
was still mid-morning.

Yet, as wonders never end, here my wheelchair was
coming to the rescue again! We were moved from the
long lines of pilgrim coming from all over the world and
quickly whisked to just a few meters from where the Pope
was seated. My son Jun provided the power to my chair.

None of us expected that the open vehicle of Pope
Francis would pass-by where we were seated. He actually
asked the driver to slow down while passing the many
seniors and disabled seating on wheelchairs. My son Jun
almost touching the Pope said, "Dad, Pope Francis and
I had eye contact and he waved at me. Feeling *ko parang
ako lang ang tinitignan nya!* (I feel he had eyes only for
me.")

I whispered to Jun, "Thank the wheelchair." I had
a feeling God has more plans for us as the pilgrimage
progresses.

That afternoon we drove to San Giovanni Retondo
to "meet" with St Padre Pio, the other saint whom the
Church acknowledges as having stigmata; the other one
is St Francis of Assisi.

Jun said, "Dad, *siguro ako puwede rin maging santo.*
(Dad, I think I too can be a saint)

"*Huh, bakit?* Why do you say so?"

"Because I am also astigmatic."

"*Har, har, har, ang mais mo.* You're corny." My son Jun is the funny one. Even when he was growing up, he and I would exchange jokes for hours. He is the life of the family and his brother and sisters... even their barkada... always want him around. Jun has a way with people, including the strangers he meets for the first time gravitate to him. Our pilgrim group felt the same about him; and as the bus carried us you could hear his infectious laughter. ...

He spent his higher education at California State University in Bakersfield. He was both a serious student and happy go lucky one. His IQ is superior and his EQ even more. He practically breezed through his undergraduate and graduate studies. As young people are apt to, they worked hard on their studies and spend their free time doing anything they want.

One time, I walked into his room with a girl crying; worried I asked what's going on. "Dad my friend won't graduate unless he submits his paper and its due on Monday. She wants my help but she has written only a few pages."

"Two days, isn't that cutting it too short? Can you do it?

"I'll see, what I can do."

That girl was jumping all over the stage when she received her diploma. That's who Jun is, couldn't say no to a friend in need.

There was a time we visited Napa Valley. As most of you are aware Napa Valley is the seat of some of the best wines in the world. Robert Mondavi founded the Winery back in 1966. It is one of the biggest winery in the valley.

Years of hard work paid off with the Medal of Honor given by L'Ordre Mondial for his accomplishment and putting America in the map of wines.

There are many interesting stories about wine raising. They say that wine raising is more difficult than raising a baby. Even if good water is available, they control the water going to the roots. But wine growers are careful that the point where the vines almost go into shock without water is not reach. Then slowly water in drips are allowed to reach the roots. This condition is maintained until the vine is ready for the grapes. The result of the process is nothing but quality wine.

In this particular trip, we were in a line were a glass of wine is available for just five dollars. But the line was long so we decided to move and saw a line with few persons nursing their glasses. We came to the bar and asked for a drink. Courteously the bar tender said. "Sir, its thirty dollars a glass."

As much as I would like to make Mondavi happy, we are not in the same league!

But the lesson I would like to leave behind; like the good wines of Napa Valley we should care for our children well, let them live in a family surrounded with love. Above all we should live within our means. For guys like us whose pocket is not bulging with money let's not pretend!

The teachings of Pope Francis is focused on the family, where Joy and laughter is the atmosphere we must nurture...

Like the life of Jesus Christ in the Holy Rosary!
GOD BLESS EVERYONE!

CHAPTER 7

Is there a Sad Christmas?

❧ ❧ ❧

*T*hat visit to Pope Francis was a year ago. Now, he is giving us two reasons to be happy with the coming Christmas and his proclamation of an Extra-Ordinary Jubilee Year.

Christmas in our family is always a time of celebration especially in 2016 when Pope Francis declared an extra-ordinary year of mercy. Pope John Paul II open the Door of Mercy in the year 2000 and the next schedule for the opening of the Holy Doors is in 2025. The Pope in his wisdom declared the extra-ordinary Jubilee because he wanted people be merciful in the light of troubles happening all over the world.

The beginning of the Jubilee Year is always solemnly marked by the opening of a Holy Door by the Pope in St. Peter's Basilica in the Vatican. However, for this Jubilee of Mercy Pope Francis also wanted a Door of Mercy in each diocese so that everyone throughout the world may be able to celebrate the Jubilee. In Lourdes, this door is at Saint Michael's gate entrance to the Sanctuary.

The tradition of a holy door during a jubilee dates back to the fifteenth century: according to the description given in 1450 by a certain Giovanni Rucellai of Viterbo, it was Pope Martin V who in 1423, at the Basilica of Saint John Lateran, opened the Holy Door for the first time in the history of the Jubilee. His successors, especially Pope Alexander VI in 1499, maintained this tradition and extended it to the four major Basilicas, namely, in addition to Saint John Lateran, the Basilica of Saint Peter in the Vatican, Saint Mary Major and Saint Paul Outside the Walls.

Before the jubilee of 2000, it was customary for the Sovereign Pontiff to open the Holy Door of Saint Peter's Basilica, and then delegate this power to a Cardinal for opening doors in the other three Basilicas. Pope John Paul II broke with that tradition by performing the opening and closing of each of these doors himself. Saint Peter's Basilica is still the first to be opened and the last to be closed.

In 1975, the ritual of closing and opening of the Holy Door was changed to better highlight the symbol of the door. In a way, until 1975, the rite emphasized the wall that prevented access, in normal times, to the Holy Door. The opening ceremony consisted of the demolition of the wall, which further emphasized the exceptional side of the Jubilee. Thus, the symbolism attached to the rite used masonry tools: a hammer to knock the wall, a trowel for building, bricks bearing inscriptions and marks of the pontificate, holy water to bless the stones and bricks, coins bearing the effigy of the Pope to allow us to date the construction of the wall of the Holy Door. The door itself consisted of two simple unadorned planks of wood.

At Christmas 1975 modifications were made to the rite of closing of the Holy Door. The Pope no longer used the trowel and bricks to begin the rebuilding of the wall, but simply closed the two sides of the bronze door. Even though the wall which enclosed the door was later rebuilt inside the Basilica, the symbolism was changed by drawing attention to the Door and away from the wall.

A door in everyday life has several functions, all repeated by the symbol of the Holy Door:

1. It marks the separation between inside and outside, between sin and the order of grace (MI 7:18-19);it permits entry to a new place, in showing mercy and not condemnation (Mt 9:13);

2. It provides protection, it provides salvation (Jn 10:7).

Jesus said: "I am the gate" (Jn 10:7). There is only one way that opens wide the entrance into the life of communion with God: this is Jesus, the one and absolute way to salvation. To him alone can the words of the Psalmist be applied in full truth: "This is the Lord's own gate: where the just may enter" (Ps 117:20).

The Holy Door reminds the faithful of their responsibility when crossing the threshold:

1. It is a decision which implies the freedom to choose, and at the same time the courage to abandon something, to leave something behind (cf. Mt 13, 44-46)

2. Passing through this door means professing that Jesus Christ is Lord, in strengthening our faith in Him to embrace the new life He has given us. This is what Pope John Paul II had announced to the world on the day of his election: "Open wide the doors to Christ".

With this short description of the JUBILEE YEAR, our family led by my daughter Leah with her children made the traditional visit in our Diocese. For perspective, our two boys and their families are residents of another country. Soon, Leah and the children will follow my son-in-law and her eldest son to make a trek to the land of milk and honey. They left as the scent of Christmas was just around the corner.

As our tradition we hear midnight mass to celebrate the birthday of our Lord.

In the homily, I heard a most touching story from Fr. Ronnie, a good friend who shared his experience when he was a much younger priest on his posting in a Chicago Parish.

It was also his first time to celebrate mass among people of another land. Immediately, he noticed that as the parishioners were trooping in everyone were bringing gifts. Wow! He thought there must be some kind of exchange gift after the mass or are they bringing those gifts for the church?

To his surprise when he stood on the door of the church to greet them as they were coming out, they handed him the gifts with a big smile, a warm welcome, and a very Merry Christmas!

His first feeling was elation with such a wonderful surprise, then, happiness for it was the first time that such load of gifts that almost filled half of his room came to him. As he was looking at the file of boxes wrapped in beautiful colors of green, red, and purple; he felt a kind of sadness, sadness because of so much bounty and no one to share it with!

Back home in Mindanao, in the little church he called home, people are as gracious as the Chicagoan's with their gifts. They brought rice cakes, and other sorts of native delicacies. Yet, they are as precious as the ones he just received from his American friends. He measured them with love rather than money. In his little church people come the whole day long and parishioners feast with those native delicacies.

I could easily relate with the feeling of sadness of Fr. Ronnie. Like him in the year of the Jubilee and Christmas, my wife and I missed our usual gift giving with Leah and her kids. We are lucky our youngest daughter Nikki and husband Watot were with us!

The meaning of this celebration date back 2000 years ago. Allow me to borrow from the gospel of St Luke (2:1-5) as he narrates the events leading to the birth of Jesus Christ: "In those days a decree went out from Caesar Augustus that the whole world should be enrolled. This was the first enrollment when Quirinius was governor of Syria. So, all went to be enrolled each to his own town."

As it has become my habit when reading any portion of the Bible, I try to transfer myself to the time of the events and make myself participant of the events as they unfold. Here then is my own experience of the first Christmas story:

There were no rooms in the Inn. Joseph tried the last place along the road. "My wife is about to give birth. We will appreciate any place. Please can you spare a room, no matter how small? Joseph beg.

The Innkeeper's wife heard Joseph's supplication. She pulled her husband aside. "The night is chilly," she said. "Why don't we let the young man and his wife use the cave below, where the animals are kept?"

Joseph did all he could to make the place as comfortable for Mary as much possible. He sat on a stone outside the cave for a long time until he heard Mary calling in a barely audible voice. Mary smiled as Joseph bent over for a better look. There, in swaddling clothes, he saw the tiny face of the infant, the Messiah.

In my mind I saw the angels singing, "Joy to the world the Lord is come....." and then I was transported among the shepherds. I was lying beside two of them. The one on my right wakeful upon the stone wall. The other sent soft moist, snoring up towards heaven.

All at once the stars began its dance. The two of us leaped to our feet. The sheep stumbled up, running in all directions. The stars countless, were flashing like white, yellow, fires against the black sky!

We all stood unable to move. We saw and heard the angel of the Lord said, "Don't be afraid; I am here to give you good news, great joy for all the people. Today a savior is born in David's town; he is the Messiah and the Lord. Let this be sign to you: You will find the baby wrapped in a swaddling clothes and lying in a manger."

At this, we stood up; the young shepherd started off; seeing him we followed. A star above kept in front of us. As we came nearer the star stood still. We were greeted with the image of a man seated on his haunches and a woman resting her head on his lap. Next to them in a stone manger is the baby swaddled in linen cloth. The young shepherd sigh, "The Messiah!"

We crept in and knelt by the first shepherd. The woman glanced up and smiled. "Mother," I said, "Your baby is the most beautiful baby I have ever seen, as soft as the nose of a lamb."

The other shepherd corrected me, "As soft as the wisp of cloud in the sky."

The baby heard us, smiled, and then closed his eyes. But his smile lingered before he finally went to sleep.

This Christmas, a feeling of sadness come to me in small doses. I felt it when two sons decided to settle in the States. I have forgotten that feeling. This year it came back like tiny pinch of pain in my heart. Our daughter with her lovely children got the bug. She saw the grass greener in the other side of the fence. Our grand kids, Marti, Luke and Christian took the plane with their mom leaving only their scents to linger on....and the sadness is back.

The Jubilee Year is a Year of Mercy. Our prayer, selfish though it maybe, is for our Nikki to stay with us, forever!

CHAPTER 8

The Faces of Mercy

❧ ❧ ❧

*F*or each person the Door of Mercy as celebrated by the Catholic Church has its own meaning. Critical for our understanding is the Church source of teaching. To the Catholics our belief is that Tradition and Scripture cannot be separated. The first gospel written by St. Mark was written 100 years after the death of Jesus Christ. His work is believed to come from St. Peter and since Mark was under the mentorship of Peter for many years it is natural that his gospel story is really from the mouth of St. Peter.

We believed that while the celebration of the Door of Mercy is quite difficult to appreciate even to Catholics an example of how one understands its meaning will help. But underneath all this is the teaching that the opening of the door of mercy is an act of love.

The Jews has been waiting for generations of a promised Messiah. They lived in suffering from the harsh rule of the Romans abetted by their own Jewish rulers. They saw Jesus as a revolutionary leader, and his crucifixion on the cross was a big disappointment.

The family of Jun and Leah in America

As Cleopas and the other disciple discussed these things on the road to Emmaus, Jesus himself came up and walked along with them; but they were kept from recognizing him. He asked them, "What are you discussing together as you walk along?" They stood still, their faces downcast. The Lord spoke of the teachings of the prophets, yet the dialogue in the gospel would be too short for that 7 miles trek to Emmaus from Jerusalem. What other things did they talked about?

I researched many written works about this event on the road to Emmaus. Numerous scholarly books and journals have been published and even renowned speakers refer to it. Yet none of what I read captures enough the powerful dialogue that took place between them.

As a writer, I can only dream of witnessing and hearing the exchange of words that took place as the two disciples walked with Jesus. And as a faithful follower, I yearn to be part of that group. What did they talk about? What could have I learned? Could it have changed who I am today?

And then it happened. I found myself standing on a dusty road and from a distance I saw three figures approaching. Cleopas and the other disciple intently listening to Kuya Hesus. It was Kuya who greeted me first. "Hi Rudy, have you been waiting long?"

"*Hindi po,* I was just here and saw you."

"Come walk with us."

I was in awe seeing them. I listened as they talked. Their exchanges centered on a lot of things, how Jesus missed his friends, the beatings more painful, as he felt the agony of Mama Mary seeing him suffer so much. Still, I did not hear any mention of why Jesus had to suffer and die. As if reading my thoughts the Lord touched my shoulder, "What are you thinking about Rudy, you've been silent?"

I was lost in my thoughts, I didn't know what to say. Then Kuya Hesus looked at me intently, with eyes penetrating. I took courage and asked, "Why did you have to suffer and die"?

He smiled, "I did it for you."

I looked down unable to keep up the conversation. "Let us not talk about me, is there something else in your mind?"

The Lord signaled us to stop. "Why don't we rest for a while? Cleopas share with us your water and let's listen to Rudy."

I looked at the Lord a bit hesitant. I glanced at Cleopas and the other disciple both smiling urging me on. "Kuya, you have given me a wonderful life, I could not have asked for anything more. I don't know but you seem to know when to test our faith. In early 2015 you took my right kidney; it's yours to take anyway, and in your goodness left me with a healthy left kidney. My doctors were amazed. The cancer gobbled half of my right kidney, yet, the cancer cells did not affect my other organs. Did you want me to do something for you Kuya?

There was sadness in his eyes, a smile too, of uncertainty, "I have plans for you but I am not sure how much you can take. You pray a lot but struggle with your faith but, parang nababawasan ang tiwala mo at nagtatampo ka na sa akin." (you seem to lose trust in me) The Lord replied.

"Kuya, in everything I do, I always pray for your guidance and I do what you want? But you know Kuya, my feeling is you don't have the same time for me anymore. I consoled myself with the thought that you must be very busy with so many of us praying for your mercy."

"Well, you may not feel my presence, but when you write, I hover over you, I wanted to make sure you share only thoughts that grow in the heart of my people. I am proud of you because every morning you go to your laptop with a weakened body. You wanted to please me and I appreciate that very much."

Kuya Hesus stood up. Cleopas and the other disciple followed. "Come Rudy, Emmaus is still a long way. Let's walk while we talk."

"Rudy, you asked me, is there something I want you to do for me? Yes, you must be prepared. You are one of those I have chosen to lighten the load of my cross. It is a different cross you will carry, yours will be the face of my mercy."

I looked at Kuya Hesus, unbelieving, my mouth open in awe. I asked him, "Lord, do you think I can do it?"

The Lord laughed. "Rudy, let me tell you the story of a simple God-fearing farmer. One of my angels appeared before him one day, and announced: "God recognizes your extraordinary righteousness. He wishes to reveal Himself to you in whatever manner you desire. How do you wish to see God?"

After a deep thought, the farmer replied, "I am but a poor farmer unworthy to see God face to face. But if He will be revealed to me, please let it be on those things I am familiar with. Let me see God in the faces of my family, my friends, my neighbors, and even my enemies, too."

"I am putting myself in the shoes of that farmer and I am asking myself, 'how do I see you Rudy?'"

"I see you in the faces of farm helpers who were all too eager to glorify and worship the Lord because you and Leth built them a chapel in your farm.

"I see you in the faces of the children in your farm, starving for education. You fed their hunger with full scholarships. And you changed the life of these children. They became the catalyst for the good.

"I see you in the faces of children living in the poorest part of your parish as you and your friends in the Knight of Columbus spearheaded the scholarship program initiated by your Parish Priest.

"I see you in the face of a former office-mate and dear friend who was cancer-stricken. You tapped into your resources for the expensive yet much needed drugs and medicines.

"I see you in the face of a friend seriously ill. You have always been ready with your check book. You provided him hospitalization and extended financial help for his family.

"I see you in the face of your lovely wife, and was constantly reassured of another blessed day.

"I see you in the faces of your children and apos, and for always, with a broad smile on your face, you and your family welcome me in your home.

"And yet, you seem to doubt the future I have for you"

"I am sorry Kuya please forgive me. I always know that in your suffering is the righteousness of Job's message – that the closer we are to you, the greater can be our suffering. I remember the words of St Teresa of Avila in one of her intense prayers in the middle of one of the episodes of her painful sufferings and you told her, "But this is how I treat my friends!"

She could only let out a deep sigh of surrender and replied: "No wonder you have so few of them!"

"Here I am offering you my whole-hearted trusting love. And today, in spite of my illness, is the height of my love for you. Higher than ever, for I always followed your words: "If you did this to the least of your brothers..." – that is who you are to me, Kuya."

We were silent. No one spoke. All of us were waiting for Kuya Hesus' words. "You must be prepared with the challenges coming your way."

I requested Cleopas for a drink of water. "I will do my best Kuya, but let me say, I am sorry if I may disappoint you."

"Don't worry, I will be with you."

Cleopas broke our conversation. "Lord, Emmaus is near."

The Lord look at me to say goodbye. I gave him a tight hug. Slowly, he held my shoulders and push a bit looking at me intently. I didn't know I was crying. "Its fine Rudy, wash your worries with your tears and do your best, be the face of my mercy."

Before he let me go, Kuya tussled my hair, "Everything is fine with us Rudy, you'll see."

And then I felt the tug of my wife, "Dad, Dad, you're dreaming. Why are you crying?

"It's alright, I will tell you tomorrow."

I look at the window and saw the light of dawn creeping and asked myself, "Am I worthy to be Kuya Hesus face of mercy?

My wife and children in Rome during the pilgrimage.

My Kuya Buddy is at the right of my mother.
This is our last family picture

CHAPTER 9

The Song I Shall Sing for You

⁂ ⁂ ⁂

"...I shall not speak
Of how I gripped death's
Wind-rung, wind-sucked throat
And heard instead, God
Singing a song to you."
(Adrian Cristobal Cruz)

The words of Kuya Hesus reverberated in my ears, "You will be the face of my Mercy."

As I look back, I saw myself in the distant years when I was slowly stepping out of Unilab. The memory of those years stayed, refuses to dissolve in the lingering dusk, instead mingled with the joys and pains of years gone by.

I saw the twilight of my career when the changing of the guards has come to fore. This must be part of God's plans, for in the change of leadership is also the beginning of a new leadership style. The past leaders managed us with deep personal touch but the trends of the present is moving towards a system of relationship that is "high tech but low touch." I worry how it will impact the mindset of people used to Amo's style, "high touch but low teach."

I heave a sigh. I recall the thoughts of friend, "to every dream there is an end. The genesis of a song presages a fall. And love which is a song is but a dream. Only memory is undying. Only divinity is life. All else is but wind, moving and unmoving—everywhere, anywhere, nowhere!"

As I took my final steps out of the gates of Unilab, I was secured in the thought that I am just moving to the next door. ... To Unilab Bayanihan Foundation. It was the thought of the academe that scared me.

I hesitated to jump ahead for fear that I may not be up to par with its demands. The nagging thought refused to leave my mind. I was actually in the recluse of the small chapel in our farm when a beautiful song joined my thoughts: *"Here I am Lord heard, is it I Lord? I have heard you calling in the night, I will go Lord if you lead me, I hold your people in my heart!"*

My face broke in innocent smile, pure, unadulterated, and full of joy. My memories flew back to lessons when children have angel's wings. Always they sing to the Lord a new song, His name they praise with dancing. I asked myself, "Childhood when will I see you again?"

As if reading my thoughts the Lord brought me back to the time before World War II broke out. Paracale is a gold mine in Camarines Sur, in the Bicol Region. Our Tatay was mechanical plant engineer of the mine. One of Tatay's passions is hunting. He owned several rifles and his favorite was the Remington rifle – every hunter's dream.

My Kuya Buddy, our eldest and Tatay often go hunting. They have these uncanny six-sense, the ability to read each other's mind. When they go on a hunt, Kuya is always a few paces behind to give Tatay chance to mark his target. As soon as his shot rang, Kuya is running having anticipated Tatay's line of fire. He never doubted Tatay would miss. It is the kind of confidence you find only in a relationship of trust and love. Walking back home Kuya with their catch on his shoulder, is the proudest, prouder than the hunter, because the townsfolk speak of how good the hound is, who never losses the hunter's catch.

There was this one time when Tatay decided to bring me along. Days before the hunt, I was the recipient of an intensive training, how to be a hound. Kuya showed me the best crouching position to keep out of the target's eye line, who could notice movements, and prevent shooing the prey away. He tested my nose for different smells. With my eyes blind folded he would run items before me, salt, ketchup, fish, meat, anything and everything that will help my sense of smell tell the difference.

And the hunt began. I was only 6 years old. The night before I couldn't sleep, I run over and over again in my mind the things Kuya taught me. Can you believe that I can hear the sound of water flowing as someone uses the bathroom and that tepid, hurting smell of urine unmistakably penetrating my senses? I was ready, I knew I was.

When we got there, I could not believe what I saw. The forest was so lush the rays of the sun could not get through. It was eerie. It was the middle of the day yet we were walking in dusk. But I was smart enough to keep this anxiety to myself. Tatay had his rifle ready, cocked, and pointing upward in case we stumble upon a rare opportunity. We were jumping over a rock in a stream when Tatay's foot suddenly slipped and accidentally pulled the rifle's trigger. We were all safe with the rifle pointing upward but we were startled by the thud we heard coming from a nearby tree.

The next thing I remember was running to the spot where the sound came from. Kuya cleared the way. As soon as he heard the sound of gunfire, his instinct looked at the direction of Tatay's rifle. He was on his way before we could even blink. To our dismay, we saw a monkey bleeding, gasping for breath, and tightly holding on to her chest, her baby crying. We were all stunned. I couldn't remember how long we stood there. But it was the monkey's struggle for last breath that awakened us from our shock.

Kuya's presence of mind spurred us to action. He was pressing something on the monkey's chest, a bunch of leaves. He was trying to stop the bleeding, the bullet hitting close to the heart. Tatay took over, told us to look for the monkey's baby.

But the baby was too fast for us. He disappeared behind the groves, probably fearing for his life. I saw how Kuya's reflexes work. Every step of the way, he was in the monkey's path not until the baby decided to climb up a tree. How could we explain that all we wanted was to care for him now that his mother was gone? We gave up. We couldn't coach the monkey to come down. He was hissing and screaming at us.

Tatay, using his own hands and a knife, dug a hole. It was big enough when we came back. And I saw how Tatay suffered. There were tears in his eyes. He wiped his face, to hide the tears. We buried the monkey and stayed for a while hoping the baby monkey would come to the scent of his mother.

That was the last time the three of us ever went hunting. And as far as I can remember, Tatay never touched his rifle again. It was on that day, at six years old, I learned how precious life is -- it didn't matter whether it is human or animal. For all of us are creatures of only one God. I guess Kuya too, knew the meaning of life.

That lesson guided me and every actions I did since then is curved in the thought that only God can take away life.

Tatay sang me the song I will always sing.

> *"...I shall not speak*
> *Of how I gripped death's*
> *Wind-rung, wind-sucked throat*
> *And heard instead, God*
> *Singing a song to you."*

For GOD is a GOD of love!

These are the guys and gals of my high school group.
Unfortunately, Maria is not in the picture.
I am on the left most in the first row.

CHAPTER 10

The Kiss that Was

❧ ❧ ❧

This is a love story of a friend in high school.

Everyone looked at Miguel as he slowly walked towards Maria. He stopped so close that they could hear the sound of each other's breathing. His hands found hers and ever so gently pulled her towards him. His lips touched her lips. She didn't know how to react. Unknowingly, she clung to him and kissed him back, a longing trembling kiss, not of passion but of goodbye.

And as Miguel stayed to envelope her in his warmth, she heard church bells ringing inside her head. She knew then that Miguel was her man. He kept holding her and wouldn't let go. Then both of them heard Mama say, "Maria, you will miss your flight. Don't worry, Miguel, she's coming back. The distance will make your hearts grow fonder." She didn't have the heart to add, "And maybe forget."

Her new home in America was the dormitory. She couldn't believe the soaring buildings. The university campus was sprawling. The buildings were apart she needed extra time to walk the distance between classrooms. Unlike in the Philippines, the method of study was different. In her country, students were fussed over by their teachers. In America, she must do things on her own. The professors only served as facilitators. They assigned readings and expected that you throw an original idea or two during class. It would be embarrassing to be called and be caught mustering words that barely made sense. It was this kind of environment that challenged Maria.

After a few months, she was ahead in her school work. Classroom life was beginning to bore her. She found herself involved in many extra-curricular activities. Her adviser tried encouraging her to take time and relax but Maria said the extra-curricular things were her way of finding relaxation. Of course, it also helped her discover more meaningful ways of immersing herself in American life.

Miguel wrote her constantly. But she didn't want him thinking there was something between them. There were times when the letter would stay in her desk unopened for several days. "I needed to keep my priorities straight," she told me. She didn't want to encourage Miguel to wait for her, though his kiss stayed in her mind. It was the kiss more than the letters that bonded her to Miguel.

While he professed his love for her, Maria never took it to its real depth. She would have preferred being told that she was beautiful and that her face was like an angel. But Miguel never said anything so shallow like that. He was always serious. "How inconsiderate of him, no, how stupid," she was looking for a stronger word to describe the apparent negligence of Miguel to say something about her being a woman. "I hope he is not taking me for granted," she mused.

But the news from Manila changed everything. Her mother was dying. She shelved her plans for a doctorate.

Cancer had befallen her mother. She was in constant pain. Without a second thought, she packed up and left for home. God, in all his wisdom, kept her mother long enough so she wouldn't suffer. She had quality life in her final days. And for the first time, she learned of the devotion Miguel showered on her mother. During those years when she was away, he had courted her mother with the same intensity he had done to her. He was her companion, driver, and everything else in between. He was the person she trusted to take her to the doctor for therapy. Her mother, too, fell in love with Miguel. On her mother's deathbed, she made a promise, "I have loved Miguel all this time, and the thought that you loved him too makes me love him even more." Though her mother missed their wedding, it was enough that when God took her, she knew that her one wish for Maria was going to come true.

Miguel was everything he said he was. He was a loving husband, always supportive and caring. He took Maria back to America. Without the support of her husband, she would not have been able to finish her doctorate degree. He freed her from the attention children needed while growing up. Sometimes guilt would haunt her; Miguel was father and mother of the children. In his unspoken ways, he was also making sure that Maria would learn to be independent in case she losses him prematurely.

But still, it came as a shock. Miguel had been complaining of having difficulty breathing. The years had added poundage to his body, his heart became incapable of carrying the load of pumping blood to the rest of his arteries. The doctors said they would have to operate. Heart bypass was now a common procedure and they could do it with their eyes closed. "Don't worry, Maria," the surgeon assured her, "we have done this procedure a thousand times."

Miguel should have been up and about the day after his surgery but his temperature was persistently above normal. Something else was making him sick. More tests were made to pinpoint the source of infection. They discovered a new virus that the hospital was unaware of. The initial report said AIDS was common among homosexuals. It was much later that they would discover that blood transfusion is also a major means of transmitting AIDS. For Miguel, it was a fatal mistake.

More than the pain of death is the experience of dying. That's because the dying person tries to prepare those he will soon leave by assuring them that death is actually a happy occasion. It is something to look forward to because it is the moment when one stands face to face with the Savior. But of course, it isn't that easy to fathom. In one of Maria's visits to the hospital, Miguel was in a pensive mood. He was already thinking of how much of a burden he had become to his wife. "I'm so sorry to make you this uncomfortable, I really didn't mean to. But all these tubes attached to my body, the constant pain, are making it difficult for me to touch you. I miss the warmth of your embrace. Sometimes, I wake up feeling scared. I feel so lost. My mind struggles to remember those tender moments we treasure so much."

Maria looked away. She couldn't bear to see Miguel hurting; then very slowly, she turned back to him and held his hand. Gathering enough strength, she whispered in his ear, "It doesn't make me uncomfortable. It's just that seeing you like this, unable to do more for you, makes me feel so helpless. Even now in your suffering, I am still your concern. You are still thinking of me."

She put down the bottle of medicine from her hands, ran her fingers through his hair, and still leaning on him asked, "Are you tired?"

"A little, I want to sleep but I don't want to miss these moments when I can keep a conversation with you. I want to be awake because I know I will have all the time to rest when the Lord finally comes to bring me home."

"Please, Miguel don't talk like that," looking away so he wouldn't see her tears. They would have a few more peaceful moments like this, remembering the love they shared, the smile in spring as roses began to bloom, the sudden rain that wet them, the dance to their love song, the hug to say goodbye, before Miguel turned to worst. And in those trying moments God gave them a life together that was not just physical, but also spiritual. They found deeper meaning in each other in the unity of their existence. They knew that anything less was a waste of God's gift, and sorrow would always be dogging their footsteps. They wanted only God's care.

Finally, Maria began to see only the beautiful memories that Miguel brought into their lives. And as always, it was their first kiss that lingered in her mind. They kissed for the last time wanting to recapture that moment. But this time, there was no more trembling. The familiarity strengthened their love. Their love gave them solitude in the absence of each other. And the memory of that last kiss was what Maria. She would not miss him. His memory would remain in her, always.

A WAY OF LOVING

Miguel and Maria met, started their life with a kiss, and finally sealed their love with a kiss. They fell in love, despite their differences. Or maybe it was their differences that led them together. Whatever it was, it must have been something rare and beautiful because that was what their love created.

Maria told me, "The kind of love Jake and I had will only happen once in this lifetime. I may fall in love again someday, yet the love I have for him will be forever. Every minute that we spent together has been sealed in my memory. I'll never forget a single moment of it, especially our first kiss. Can I share with you the dream I had last night?"

"Of course," I replied.

"Last night, Miguel visited me in my dream. He knows this pain I carry with me just wouldn't go away," she paused still overwhelmed by what happened. "The reason why it hurts so much, he said to me in my dream, was because our souls are connected."

"And then Miguel said, 'Do you remember how we would suddenly sing the same tune, break out the same lines, and laugh our hearts out because we seem able to read each other's mind? Maybe it's because our souls have always been connected that's why being apart is breaking our hearts now. This goodbye that we have, my leaving ahead of you, has become a goodbye to a part of our own selves and a welcome to a new beginning. And for reasons we will never understand, it just had to happen. But I promise you, we will find each other again and make up for the times we missed.' "

Maria was in tears. It felt so real in her dream. Even now it still felt real and vivid. She knew in her heart Miguel might be physically away but his spirit would continue to protect, guide, and love her.

A few days after, Maria was on the phone. She said she was now beginning to let go though aware that it might take some time. She thanked me profusely.

I know their love will never die!

God is a God of Second Chances

✍ ✍ ✍

As I write these final pages, God gave me another lease in life. My doctor said, "You are responding well to my medication"

Life is a never-ending cycle and change is always part of life. The effect of change maybe positive or negative. It may bring joy or sadness. It is a process of life. The poet T.S. Eliot said, " I had seen birth and death but had thought they were different." Accepting that all things have a beginning and end, my realization is: we should be discerning in search of our own quest of what life brings, for at the end of the day they are all priceless gifts from our Lord.

To me, the end purpose of life is the acquisition of wisdom that enlightens the mind, one that enables the spirit to embrace the most diffcult quest...love of neighbor that leave us with peace of mind.... Is there a goal higher than that?

Toltec wisdom teaches that "The sad part is that people live their lives and never discover that the judge and the victim rule their minds. There is need to take the first steps to personal freedom and that is to be aware of the problems comfronting us in order to solve the same problem. Let us be aware that everyday we wake up charged with a certain amount of mental, emotional, and physical energy that we spend throughout the day. If we allow our emotions to deplete that energy, we have nothing left to **change our life to make it worth living for others**. Now, that is what love is all about.

The sun is setting for many of us as we stand on the hill overlooking life. In the gathering darkness, we lit candles to guide our way back to what should be. It is the end of the a day, full of meaning, a day that started with a promise and to many delivered on that promise.

Imagine me, holding my wife's hand tightly. The moon hung over the horizon as countless stars hanging high above the hill. The cold slow, its timed to our breathing, Leth leaned her head on my shoulder, and as if on cue, we whispered to each other, "Kuya Hesus keep us always in your embrace..."

Suddenly the wind swept up the hill and sang the final message, "You are to live clean and pure, like children of God. Shine like beacon lights, but always feel my love. I will keep you in my embrace as I give you a second chance in life."

Made in the USA
Middletown, DE
17 May 2017